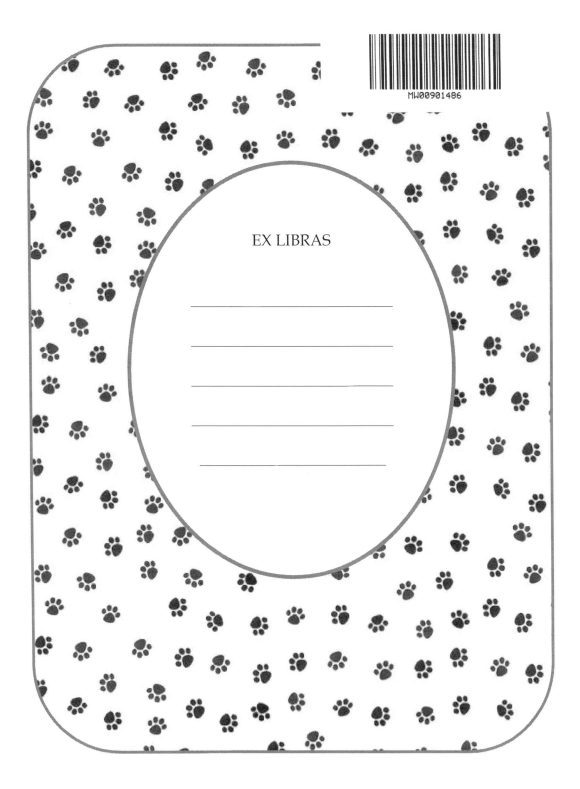

EX LIBRAS

Other Titles in the
SO CUTE PUPPY SERIES

If dogs could talk,
it would take a lot
of the fun out of
owning one.
- Andy Rooney

Some angels choose
fur instead of wings.
- Jennifer Skiff

_____
_____
_____
_____
_____
_____
_____
_____
_____
_____
_____
_____
_____
_____
_____

In order to keep a true perspective of one's importance, everyone should have a dog that will worship him and a cat that will ignore him.

- Dereke Bruce

Did you ever notice when you blow in a dog's face he gets mad at you? But when you take him in a car he sticks his head out the window.
- *Steve Bluestone*

Amount of time it takes for a dog to "do its business" is directly proportional to outside temperature + suitability of owner's outerwear.
- *Betsy Cañas Garmon*

The reason a dog has so many friends is that he wags his tail instead of his tongue.

- Author Unknown

Anybody who
doesn't know what
soap tastes like
never washed a
dog.
- *Franklin P. Jones*

The dog is a
gentleman; I hope to
go to his heaven,
not man's.
- Mark Twain

The difference
between friends and
pets is that friends
we allow into our
company, pets we
allow into our
solitude.
- Robert Brault

No matter how little
money and how
few possessions
you own, having a dog
makes you feel rich.
- *Louis Sabin*

My little dog- a heartbeat
at my feet.
- Edith Wharton

To sit with a dog on a hillside on a glorious afternoon is to be back in Eden, where doing nothing was not boring- it was peace.
- Milan Kundera

I really love pets. They're like children. They know if you really love them or not. You can't fool them.
- Donna Douglas

A dog teaches a boy fidelity,
perseverance, and to turn around
three times before lying down.
- Robert Benchley

Such short little lives
our pets have to
spend with us, and
they spend most of it
waiting for us to
come home each day.
- *Unknown*

A house is not a home
without a pet.
- Unknown

A dog reflects the family life. Whoever saw a frisky dog in a gloomy family, or a sad dog in a happy one? Snarling people have snarling dogs, dangerous people have dangerous ones.
- *Arthur Conan Doyle*

If you think dogs can't count, try putting three dog biscuits in your pocket and then giving Fido only two of them.
- *Phil Pastoret*

Dogs feel very
strongly that they
should always go
with you in the car,
in case the need
should arise for
them to bark
violently at
nothing right in
your ear.
- Dave Barry

To err is human, to
forgive canine.
- *Anonymous*

The great pleasure of a dog is that you may make a fool of
yourself with him and not only will he not scold you, but he
will make a fool of himself too.

- Samuel Butler

I'm totally suspicious
of people who don't
like dogs; but I totally
trust a dog when it
doesn't like a person.
- *Anonymous*

Blessed is the person who has
earned the love of an old dog.
- *Sydney Jeanne Seward*

I think dogs are
the most amazing
creatures; they
give unconditional
love. For me they
are the role model
for being alive.
- *Gilda Radner*

My goal in life is to be as good of a person my dog already thinks I am.
- *Author Unknown*

Scratch a dog and you'll find
a permanent job.
- Franklin P. Jones

Ever wonder where you'd
end up if you took your dog
for a walk and never once
pulled back on the leash?
- *Robert Brault*

There is no psychiatrist
in the world like a
puppy licking your face.
- Bernard Williams

> In order to really enjoy a dog, one doesn't merely try to train him to be semi human. The point of it is to open oneself to the possibility of becoming partly a dog.
> - *Edward Hoagland*

Dogs have a way of finding
the people who need them,
and filling an emptiness we
didn't ever know we had.

- Thom Jones

I think we are drawn to dogs because they are the uninhibited creatures we might be if we weren't certain we knew better. They fight for honor at the first challenge, make love with no moral restraint, and they do not for all their marvelous instincts appear to know about death. Being such wonderfully uncomplicated beings, they need us to do their worrying.
- George Bird Evans

Old age means realizing
you will never own all
the dogs you wanted to.
- *Joe Gores*

It's not the size of the
dog in the fight;
it's the size of the
fight in the dog.
- *Mark Twain*

> Pet hair is the new
> black.
> *- Anonymous*

Dogs have given us their
absolute all. We are the
center of their universe. We
are the focus of their love and
faith and trust. They serve us
in return for scraps. It is
without a doubt the best deal
man has ever made.
- Roger Caras

Our perfect companions never have fewer than four feet.
- *Colette*

Whoever said you can't buy happiness forgot little puppies.

- Gene Hill

You can say any
fool thing to a dog,
and the dog will
give you this look
that says, My God,
you're RIGHT I
NEVER would've
thought of that'
- Dave Barry

I wonder what goes through his mind when he
sees us peeing in his water bowl.
- *Penny Ward Moser*

Properly trained, a man can
be dog's best friend.
- Corey Ford

Dogs are the leaders of the planet. If you see two life forms, one of them is making a poop, the other one's carrying it for him, who would you assume is in charge.

- Jerry Seinfeld

The most affectionate creature in the
world is a wet dog.
- Ambrose Bierce

Pets have more love and compassion
in them than most humans.
- Robert Wagner

A dog can express more with his tail in seconds than his owner can express with his tongue in hours.
- *Author Unknown*

It's good to be around pets.
They kind of put things into perspective. They're easygoing,
loyal, and they seem to get it, even when humans don't.
- Alyson Stoner

No matter how little money and how few possessions
you own, having a dog makes you rich.
- Louis Sabin

The dog was created especially for children. He is the god of frolic.
- Henry Ward Beecher

My dogs have been the reason I
have woken up every single day of
my life with a smile on my face.
- Jennifer Skiff

The journey of life is sweeter
when traveled with a dog.
- *Anonymous*

A dog is one of the
remaining reasons
why some people
can be persuaded
to go for a walk.
- O.A. Battista

_____

_____

_____

_____

_____

_____

_____

_____

_____

_____

_____

My mother and dad were big animal lovers, too. I just don't know how I would have lived without animals around me. I'm fascinated by them - both domestic pets and the wild community. They just are the most interesting things in the world to me, and it's made such a difference in my lifetime.

- Betty White

A door is what a dog is perpetually
on the wrong side of.
- Ogden Nash

Dogs do speak, but only to those who know how to listen.
- Orhan Pamuk

I'm not a greedy man; there really is nothing I couldn't live without. But if there was a fire, and I saved my child and my pets, I'd be happy.
- Kid Rock

14685351R00062

Made in the USA
San Bernardino, CA
02 September 2014